# Wicked Problems: What Can Local Governments Do?

Eric M. Reese
Maureen M. Berner

UNC
SCHOOL OF
GOVERNMENT

The School of Government at the University of North Carolina at Chapel Hill works to improve the lives of North Carolinians by engaging in practical scholarship that helps public officials and citizens understand and improve state and local government. Established in 1931 as the Institute of Government, the School provides educational, advisory, and research services for state and local governments. The School of Government is also home to a nationally ranked graduate program in public administration and specialized centers focused on information technology and environmental finance.

As the largest university-based local government training, advisory, and research organization in the United States, the School of Government offers up to 200 courses, webinars, and specialized conferences for more than 12,000 public officials each year. In addition, faculty members annually publish approximately 50 books, manuals, reports, articles, bulletins, and other print and online content related to state and local government. Each day that the General Assembly is in session, the School produces the *Daily Bulletin Online*, which reports on the day's activities for members of the legislature and others who need to follow the course of legislation.

The Master of Public Administration Program is offered in two formats. The full-time, two-year residential program serves up to 60 students annually. In 2013 the School launched MPA@UNC, an online format designed for working professionals and others seeking flexibility while advancing their careers in public service. The School's MPA program consistently ranks among the best public administration graduate programs in the country, particularly in city management. With courses ranging from public policy analysis to ethics and management, the program educates leaders for local, state, and federal governments and nonprofit organizations.

Operating support for the School of Government's programs and activities comes from many sources, including state appropriations, local government membership dues, private contributions, publication sales, course fees, and service contracts. Visit www.sog.unc.edu or call 919.966.5381 for more information on the School's courses, publications, programs, and services.

Michael R. Smith, Dean
Thomas H. Thornburg, Senior Associate Dean
Frayda S. Bluestein, Associate Dean for Faculty Development
L. Ellen Bradley, Associate Dean for Programs and Marketing
Johnny Burleson, Associate Dean for Development
Todd A. Nicolet, Associate Dean for Operations
Bradley G. Volk, Associate Dean for Administration

FACULTY

| | | | |
|---|---|---|---|
| Whitney Afonso | Richard D. Ducker | Christopher B. McLaughlin | Jessica Smith |
| Trey Allen | Joseph S. Ferrell | Kara A. Millonzi | Meredith Smith |
| Gregory S. Allison | Alyson A. Grine | Jill D. Moore | Carl W. Stenberg III |
| David N. Ammons | Norma Houston | Jonathan Q. Morgan | John B. Stephens |
| Ann M. Anderson | Cheryl Daniels Howell | Ricardo S. Morse | Charles Szypszak |
| Maureen Berner | Jeffrey A. Hughes | C. Tyler Mulligan | Shannon H. Tufts |
| Mark F. Botts | Willow S. Jacobson | Kimberly L. Nelson | Vaughn Mamlin Upshaw |
| Michael Crowell | Robert P. Joyce | David W. Owens | Aimee N. Wall |
| Leisha DeHart-Davis | Diane M. Juffras | LaToya B. Powell | Jeffrey B. Welty |
| Shea Riggsbee Denning | Dona G. Lewandowski | William C. Rivenbark | Richard B. Whisnant |
| Sara DePasquale | Adam Lovelady | Dale J. Roenigk | |
| James C. Drennan | James M. Markham | John Rubin | |

Printed in the United States of America

18 17 16 15 14    1 2 3 4 5

ISBN 978-1-56011-761-2

∞ This publication is printed on permanent, acid-free paper in compliance with the North Carolina General Statutes.

♻ Printed on recycled paper

# About the Series

*Local Government Board Builders* offers local elected leaders practical advice on how to effectively lead and govern. Each of the booklets in this series provides a topic overview, and many offer specific tips on effective practice, worksheets, and reflection questions to help local elected leaders improve their work. The series focuses on common activities for local governing boards, such as selecting and appointing committees and advisory boards, planning for the future, making better decisions, improving board accountability, and effectively engaging stakeholders in public decisions.

Vaughn Mamlin Upshaw, lecturer in public administration and government at the UNC School of Government, is the series editor.

## Other Books in This Series

*Leading Your Governing Board: A Guide for Mayors and County Board Chairs*, Vaughn Mamlin Upshaw, 2009

*A Model Code of Ethics for North Carolina Local Elected Officials*, A. Fleming Bell, II, 2010

*Creating and Maintaining Effective Local Government Citizen Advisory Committees*, Vaughn Mamlin Upshaw, 2010

*Working with Nonprofit Organizations*, Margaret Henderson, Lydian Altman, Suzanne Julian, Gordon P. Whitaker, and Eileen R. Youens, 2010

*Public Outreach and Participation*, John B. Stephens, Ricardo S. Morse, and Kelley T. O'Brien, 2011

*Local Government Revenue Sources in North Carolina*, Kara A. Millonzi, 2011

*Getting the Right Fit: The Governing Board's Role in Hiring a Manager*, Vaughn Mamlin Upshaw, John A. Rible IV, and Carl W. Stenberg, 2011

*The Property Tax in North Carolina*, Christopher B. McLaughlin, 2012

*Local Government Budgeting: A Guide for North Carolina Elected Officials,*
Julie M. Brenman with Gregory S. Allison, 2013

*Handbook for North Carolina Mayors and Council Members,* David M. Lawrence, 2013

*How Are We Doing? Evaluating Manager and Board Performance,*
Vaughn Mamlin Upshaw, 2014

*Suggested Rules of Procedure for the Board of County Commissioners,* Joseph S. Ferrell,
Third Edition, 2002

*Suggested Rules of Procedure for Small Local Government Boards,* A. Fleming Bell, II,
Second Edition, 1998

*Suggested Rules of Procedure for a City Council,* A. Fleming Bell, II, Third Edition, 2000

# Contents

**Acknowledgments**  vii

**Introduction**  1

**Getting Started**  3
>   **Defining Wicked Problems**  3
>   **Identifying Wicked Problems**  4
>   **Making Wicked Problems More Manageable**  6
>   **Addressing Wicked Problems**  7

**Guiding Principles for Addressing Wicked Problems**  11
>   **Guiding Principle Number 1:** *You don't govern alone. Work across boundaries*
>      *to maximize all available resources.*  11
>   **Guiding Principle Number 2:** *Government is well positioned to be a convener of efforts.*  17
>   **Guiding Principle Number 3:** *Aim to shrink the problem and be willing to adjust over time.*  21

**Planning to Address Wicked Problems**  25
>   **Envision**  26
>   **Enact**  30
>   **Evaluate**  34

**Conclusion**  39

**Additional Resources**  41

**Appendix A: Defining (or Redefining) Mutual Expectations in a Collaborative Relationship**  43

**Appendix B: Wicked Problems Mapped to Stages of Strategic Planning**  45

**Appendix C: Hunger Resources**  47

# Acknowledgments

Addressing wicked problems requires coordinated effort from a variety of stakeholders. Writing about wicked problems is no different. Many people helped us produce this guidebook, and we offer our sincere appreciation for their assistance. Attempting to list all of those who influenced the final product will certainly exclude some deserving people. Nonetheless, we will try.

Many thanks to Lydian Altman, Carl Stenberg, Aimee Wall, and Jill Moore at the School of Government for providing insights to improve the content of the guidebook. We also could not have gotten to the finish line without the assistance and guidance of Nancy Dooly, Katrina Hunt, Kevin Justice, Daniel Soileau, Leslie Watkins, and Lisa Wright in the Publications Division at the School of Government. Our reviewers helped us refine the final product, and thanks go to Christy Shi, Leslie Hossfeld, Gwen Burton, and Grant Goings for taking time from their already busy lives to give critical feedback. Finally, Margaret Henderson and Vaughn Upshaw were absolutely essential to the completion of this guidebook. Margaret's ideas and encouragement on how to describe complex concepts simply and Vaughn's guidance and insight on how to structure the content enabled us to build what we hope is a useful and thorough final product. For all the assistance we received, we are sincerely grateful.

Eric M. Reese
Maureen M. Berner
Chapel Hill
Summer 2014

# Introduction

Local government leaders face a variety of problems in doing the work of local government. Addressing issues ranging from public education, water supply, and law enforcement to housing, transportation, and poverty, local government leaders must use different approaches and resources in order to act in the best interest of their communities. With so many existing responsibilities, taking on additional work while keeping a balanced budget is difficult for local governments.

In addition, despite the capacity of local governments to address community issues, some problems are difficult to solve and remain entrenched over time. The root causes of these problems are often obscure and can remain untreated even though major resources and efforts are devoted to relieving their symptoms. These persistent challenges are "wicked" problems, and they continue to drain resources and threaten the vitality of communities. Without committed action by local governments, these problems have the potential to devastate communities over time.

Yet the burden of addressing wicked problems does not fall solely on local governments. Many entities dedicate their time and resources to combating wicked problems. However, independent efforts are usually not enough to have a great effect on these complex issues. Any successful action to address them requires coordination among various groups.

Local governments are well positioned to play a leading role in a coordinated effort of this kind. Due to their proximity to constituents, their ability to plan for the long term, and their relationships with businesses, nonprofits, and other governments, local governments have a unique opportunity to help combat wicked problems. Whether operating programs to serve constituents directly, leading coordinated efforts between governments and nonprofits, or convening groups of interested citizens, local governments can work with their communities to maximize resources and take meaningful actions.

All communities face wicked problems. Issues such as pollution, poverty, and hunger do not observe boundaries, and they affect every community to some degree. Local governments need to arm themselves with strategies to combat these and other problems. This guidebook aims to equip local government leaders with tools to develop new approaches to identifying, understanding, and addressing complex issues. With these tools, local governments can take simple steps to address wicked problems in their communities.

# Getting Started

Local governments face problems in a variety of areas and in all shapes and sizes. Some problems require short-term plans and are easily solved through decisive action. Others require long-term planning and must be addressed over a period of years. In order to determine what steps to take, governments must identify problems, decide whether action is necessary, and determine the type of action that will best address the problem.

For wicked problems, figuring out where to start is a challenge. This section provides a definition of wicked problems, outlines ways to identify them, and suggests structures for strategic action to reduce their impact.

## Defining Wicked Problems

The first definition of "wicked" in a dictionary usually involves something that is morally wrong. Further down in the entry, terms such as "severe," "unjustifiable," and "beyond reason" often appear. The definition of wicked problems used in this guidebook involves these latter terms and refers to issues that have no simple solutions. Other disciplines might call these issues "systems problems," "complex problems," or "adaptive problems." They are called wicked problems throughout this book for the sake of clarity and consistency, but wicked problems could also include these other terms for problems that require complex, coordinated, long-term solutions instead of quick fixes.

Generally, wicked problems have three distinctive characteristics.[1] They are unstructured, cross-cutting, and relentless, as defined below:

- *Unstructured*. The causes and effects of wicked problems are difficult to identify. There is little consensus on the definition of the problem, and even when stakeholders agree on the issue, they may not agree on how to address it.

---

1. This definition of wicked problems comes from Edward P. Weber and Anne M. Khademian, "Wicked Problems, Knowledge Challenges, and Collaborative Capacity Builders in Network Settings," *Public Administration Review,* March/April 2008, 336–37.

- *Cross-cutting.* Wicked problems affect stakeholders from a variety of sectors, and independent action often is not productive. Engaging diverse stakeholders and coordinating efforts are critical to addressing wicked problems.
- *Relentless.* Societies cannot solve wicked problems in the traditional sense. Wicked problems may be mitigated or minimized, but they will not go away. They require long-term strategies and continuity of action.

The above characteristics distinguish wicked problems from those that are more technical in nature. For example, repairing a sewer leak is a technical problem that engineers know how to solve. It may be expensive, but with some expertise and equipment, the leak can be fixed. In contrast, implementing a wastewater system that efficiently meets the needs of local industries and growing populations without damaging the environment and drinking water supply is a much more complex problem. It requires input from a variety of stakeholders with differing goals, and it involves action over a long period of time.

Once local governments have learned to recognize the characteristics of wicked problems, they can begin to identify specific issues to address.

### Defining Hunger as a Wicked Problem

Hunger has all three characteristics of a wicked problem. It is difficult to define—people have differing opinions on what constitutes hunger and how it should be addressed. It is cross-cutting—hunger exists in all communities and affects many other issues, including education and economic development. It is relentless—hunger persists over time, and short-term efforts to address it are ineffective.

*This guidebook uses the example of hunger in North Carolina to show how local communities are addressing one wicked problem.*

## Identifying Wicked Problems

Local governments learn about concerns that must be addressed in their constituencies in a variety of ways, including issues raised on the national level, requests from constituents, mandates from the state or federal government, news stories, and community data. Wicked problems may be identified in the same ways.

Local governments can use their proximity to constituents to unearth wicked problems that state and federal governments might miss. Because of their smaller size, they may be able to identify conditions and changes in their communities that indicate wicked

## Identifying Hunger as a Wicked Problem: Free and Reduced Meals Rates for North Carolina Students, 1998–2012

**Percentage of Students Eligible for Free and Reduced Meals in North Carolina**

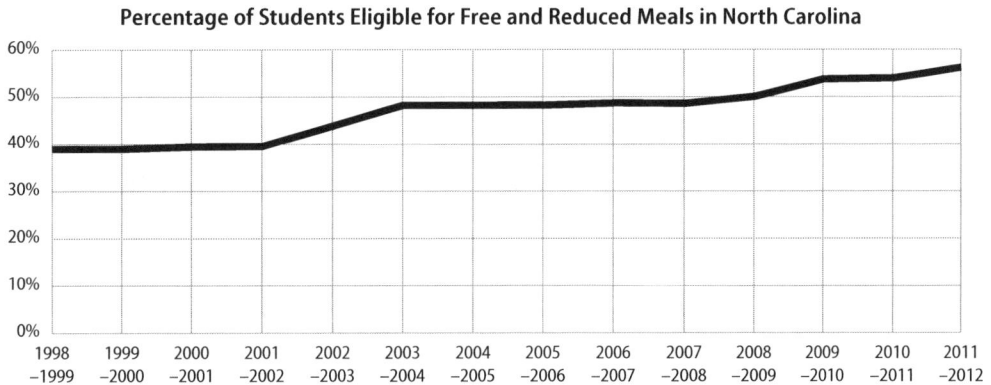

*Source*: The Annie E. Casey Foundation, KIDS COUNT Data Center, http://datacenter.kidscount.org.

One way to identify wicked problems is through traditionally collected data. The Free and Reduced Meals rate is one such measure and is a practical and measurable indicator of poverty and hunger.[a] The rate measures the percentage of children eligible for school meals assistance in each school system. Federal income guidelines allow households to become eligible for free or reduced-price school meals for their children based on their income levels.

The steady increase in the number of students eligible for free and reduced-price meals in North Carolina since 1998 shows that the relentless problem of hunger was present long before the recession of 2008.

_____

a. For a comprehensive discussion of the Free and Reduced Meals Program, see the Federal Education Budget Project at http://febp.newamerica.net/background-analysis/federal-school-nutrition-programs.

problems more quickly and easily than other levels of government. Using a variety of data, a local government can put together a full picture of an underlying problem in a community and develop strategies to address it.

Gathering data in a variety of forms from many sources is critical to determining which wicked problems are ripe for action. Traditional data, such as state and federal income statistics, are one common way to identify wicked problems. Other sources of information, however—such as appeals for donations to meet increasing demand from local nonprofits—are no less valid. It is important to make use of information from all kinds of sources.

Nonprofits and volunteer groups are useful sources of ideas to combat wicked problems, and engaging them in efforts is critical. *Location*: White Oak Ecumenical Outreach Ministries—Swansboro, NC. *Source*: *Feeding Our State—A Portrait of Hunger in North Carolina.*

## Making Wicked Problems More Manageable

Making wicked problems more manageable is critical to taking steps to combat the problems. After gathering data that suggest that a wicked problem is present, local governments can work on breaking the wicked problem into more actionable issues. For example, a government trying to address pollution might identify stormwater runoff or air pollution from a factory as a more manageable issue to combat than the wicked problem of climate change. A government dealing with infrastructure issues might identify increased public transportation options as the most practical way to tackle the problem.

There may be one aspect of a wicked problem that particularly affects a local community, or there may be many. Whether it is best to address one or more aspects is a choice that must be made locally by interested groups. Often, strategies that address the needs of more than one group help keep more people involved and interested in the solution. In any case, once a local government has identified actionable issues, it can begin to plan innovative strategies that will meet the specific needs of the community.

## Making Hunger a Manageable Problem

In the abstract, hunger is a very difficult, if not impossible, problem to combat. It has a variety of causes, and it affects different people in different ways. However, breaking the problem down into specific issues makes hunger easier to address. Leaders at the state and local level in North Carolina used data to identify children as particularly vulnerable to hunger. They then noted that children are at an increased risk for hunger over the summer without school meals. Specifically,

- Children are especially vulnerable to hunger. Over 800,000 children in North Carolina received free or reduced-price school meals throughout the 2012–2013 school year. Hunger is a problem for every community. No school district has fewer than 25 percent of students eligible for free or reduced-price meals, and in some districts, more than 90 percent of students are eligible.[a]
- Children are more at risk for hunger over the summer, when schools are not providing meals. Only about 12 percent of students eligible for free and reduced-price meals receive meals over the summer, and some areas of the state provide no meals during those months.

Breaking the problem down in this way gave state and local leaders a manageable way to combat hunger by providing meals to needy children over the summer.

a. North Carolina Department of Public Instruction, SY12–13 Free and Reduced Meals Application Data. For more information, see the department's website at www.ncpublicschools.org/fbs/resources/data.

## Addressing Wicked Problems

Wicked problems resist simple solutions. Complex planning, long-term strategies, and an ability to coordinate work across silos are needed to make measurable progress. But that does not mean that local governments should not try to address wicked problems in their communities. Local governments can be centers of innovation to tackle wicked problems, and they can work with other communities by combining resources and sharing successful strategies.

Each dimension of a wicked problem presents challenges but also opportunities. *Unstructured* problems allow local governments to create specific frameworks for attacking them. *Cross-cutting* problems allow local governments to focus on areas where resources are strongest or need is greatest. And *relentless* problems present opportunities for local governments to collaborate with others who have a shared interest in long-term community well-being.

Using well-known methods to build understanding can help various stakeholders create a common definition of the problem and allow them to take the first step in addressing it. Board committees, community input groups, and brainstorming sessions are familiar ways of convening stakeholders and creating impetus for action. In addition, taking advantage

## Planning for Action on Summer Meals

### The Background

North Carolina administers two programs that give federal reimbursements to local school districts and nonprofits that provide summer meals for children. The programs are administered by the state Department of Public Instruction and Department of Health and Human Services, respectively. Essentially, two similar programs with federal funding, state administration, and local implementation exist to address the same wicked problem.[a]

### The Conversation

The action conversation began when a statewide nonprofit brought together the state administrators of the two programs, along with some local nonprofit and school personnel, simply to talk about how the programs were run and to see if there were any obvious ways to improve them. It quickly became apparent that the two programs were parallel, but each had separate advantages. One program had less paperwork because it was administered by schools, which already had established credentials with the federal government and a structure that existed during the school year. The other program, however, had higher reimbursement rates for the meals served to each child because it was administered by nonprofits, which needed additional help to set up the summer-only program. With state leaders and local actors at the table, it was suddenly easier to ask the obvious question: Why not combine the programs in a way that results in less paperwork and higher reimbursements for all?

The group noted the following key points:

- Two federal summer meals programs are underutilized, meaning that school districts and nonprofits can potentially expand their efforts with most costs covered by federal reimbursements.
- Local school districts and nonprofits work through those programs to provide meals over the summer to eligible students.
- These parallel programs could be combined to capture the advantages of each program.

Details of the plan that resulted from this conversation are described in later sidebars.

---

a. Legislation passed in 2014 transfers the North Carolina Summer Food Service Program from the Department of Health and Human Services to the Department of Public Instruction, placing both programs under the same roof for the first time. The change is effective October 1, 2014. S.L. 2014-100 (S 744), sec. 12E.9.(a)–(b).

of a variety of perspectives can help local governments grasp the breadth of problems and single out specific issues that align with local capacity to act.

Due to their relentless nature, wicked problems require a long-term approach. They also require adaptation and constant attention throughout the process of addressing them. Local governments and their leaders can play a major role by listening to stakeholder feedback, providing resources and support, facilitating dialogue, and creating polices that enable stakeholders to maintain momentum.

The next section discusses guiding principles for addressing wicked problems.

What are some problems in your community that meet the definition of wicked problems? Who is affected by these problems?

_____

_____

_____

What wicked problems does your organization currently address? What role does your organization play in helping mitigate wicked problems?

_____

_____

_____

What data do you have about these problems in your community? How well do you feel they represent the actual situation?

_____

_____

_____

What other data could you gather to help you understand the problem? Which key people can give you more information?

_____

_____

_____

What programs does your community have, both inside and outside your organization, to address these problems? How well do you think they are working?

_____

_____

_____

# Guiding Principles for Addressing Wicked Problems

In addressing wicked problems, governments must depart from the way of thinking used to solve technical problems. Quick, direct action is not enough to combat wicked problems—local governments must create thorough, long-term plans of action. While this is difficult, it leads to better outcomes for communities.

This section outlines three basic principles to help local governments get to the heart of wicked problems. Each principle addresses the unstructured, cross-cutting, and relentless nature of these problems.

## ▶ Guiding Principle Number 1: *You don't govern alone. Work across boundaries to maximize all available resources.*

The unstructured nature of wicked problems can be frustrating for those attempting to take action. Identifying all of the resources available to attack a problem can be challenging, but it also creates an opportunity to develop a course of action that makes the most sense at the local level. Each community must determine the best strategy given local resources and constraints. In that way, each community will be able to maintain control over its own actions.

One of the greatest challenges for governments attempting to address any problem is determining who should be involved in the effort to address the issue. Many questions typically arise. Does a federal or state program already exist to address the problem? If so, can local government work with its sponsors to make the program more effective? Should the local government create its own program? Can local government collaborate with the nonprofit and business sectors to address the problem? How can constituents become involved?

To answer such questions, local governments need to determine who cares about an issue and why that person or entity is interested in addressing it. Gathering input from all

## Tailoring Programs to Local Needs and Resources

Successful strategies to address wicked problems are likely to be those that are tailored to the local situation and the resources of local partners. Delivering food to hungry kids in the summer is a good example of the need to consider local conditions and possible local partners.

A food distribution system needs to reach as many children as possible as efficiently as possible. In most cases, that means taking the food to places where kids congregate. In one community, the largest gathering place for children in need of summer meals may be a local nonprofit, such as the Boys and Girls Club. In another, the highest need may be in an area populated by families of agricultural workers. In yet another, the children may be spread along a winding road in a mountainous area. Parks and recreation programs, swimming pools, and libraries are also locations that attract children in the summer.

What is noteworthy about these locations is their diversity—some are governed by a municipality or county, while others are under the auspices of nonprofits and other organizations. This means that potential partners with a variety of resources, from ideas to volunteers to funding, exist in many areas of the community, and a program can be tailored to take advantage of such diversity.

parts of the community is critical. It can help the local government identify a wide range of potential partners and assess the motivations of those partners. Leaders can then identify how interests align and when to involve various groups.

In addition, thinking about wicked problems both vertically and horizontally can help a local government identify the players to involve. Thinking vertically, a local government may seek to collaborate with other levels of government, such as county, regional, state, or federal partners who are interested in addressing the problem. Thinking horizontally, local governments may seek to engage nonprofits, businesses, and religious institutions that can bring resources to the table. These groups may also have vertical partners who can help. Finally, local governments may want to combine forces with neighboring local governments in order to take advantage of larger opportunities to address wicked problems.

Local governments occupy a central location among potential players. This key position allows them to facilitate action, present barriers to action, or step away completely. Central positioning also gives local governments freedom to choose strategies to address wicked problems that are unique to their communities' strengths and needs.

To combat the unstructured nature of wicked problems, it is important for a local government to create a structure that addresses its needs and highlights its strengths. Any guiding structure can be completely customized to a local community. For example, in dealing with transportation issues, one local government might focus on public works to widen roads, while another might emphasize planning and developing a public transportation system or helping businesses create incentives for workers to carpool. Customizing

## Coordinating Stakeholders for Summer Meals

Providing summer meals for students in North Carolina is a complex project involving all levels of governments and a variety of nongovernment partners, as illustrated by the chart below. The US Department of Agriculture (USDA) provides funding to two oversight state agencies that provide training, instruction, and inspections at the local level and verify reimbursement submissions to the USDA. The North Carolina Department of Public Instruction (DPI) is the agency that oversees summer meal programs where the local administrative partner is a school, and the North Carolina Department of Health and Human Services (DHHS) is the agency that oversees summer meal programs where the local administrative partner is a nonprofit.[a]

At the same time, a national nonprofit, Share Our Strength, serves in a support role. It works through its own state-level organization, NC No Kid Hungry, which in turn works with everyone involved at both the state and local levels to provide supplementary financial support, materials, and information.

In some places in North Carolina, local government is part of this overall process, but in most communities, it is not. Local government is uniquely positioned to play a coordinating role among the various groups and bring a variety of resources to the table.

|  | Government | | Nonprofit |
|---|---|---|---|
| **National** | US Department of Agriculture<br>Food and Nutrition Services – Child Nutrition Programs | | Share Our Strength<br>(No Kid Hungry) |
| **State** | NC Department of<br>Public Instruction | NC Department of Health<br>and Human Services | NC No Kid Hungry |
|  |  | County and City Government | Regional Food Banks |
| **Local** | Local School District | | Faith-Based Nonprofits<br>Housing Complexes |

a. Legislation passed in 2014 transfers the North Carolina Summer Food Service Program from the Department of Health and Human Services to the Department of Public Instruction, placing both programs under the same roof for the first time. The change is effective October 1, 2014. S.L. 2014-100 (S 744), sec. 12E.9.(a)–(b).

## Food Policy Councils and Food Systems

Addressing hunger does not always mean directly distributing food. Food policy councils are one way in which groups address local food system needs, and in the process, address hunger as well.

Food policy councils are local or regionally organized groups that develop strategies and make policy recommendations to cultivate local food economies and increase access to local, healthy food. To do this, some local food policy councils have begun thinking in terms of local food systems. The diagram below shows the elements of a food system.

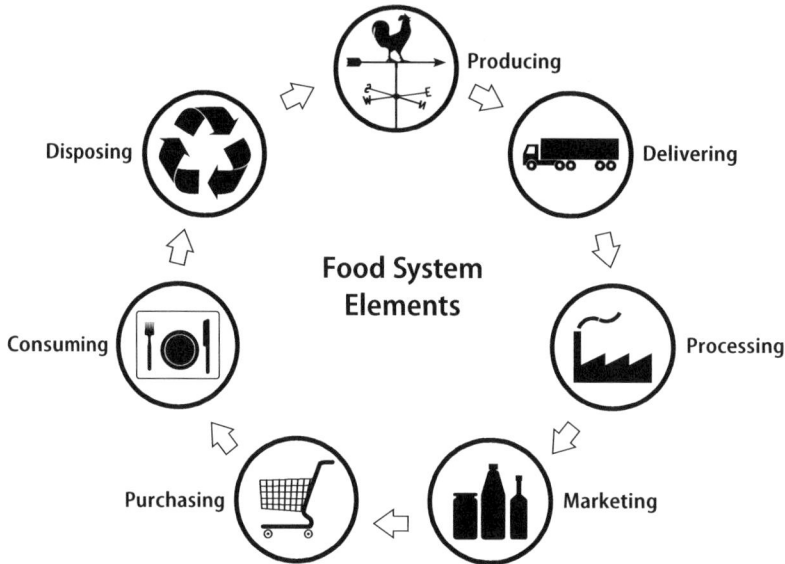

**Food System Elements**

- Producing
- Delivering
- Processing
- Marketing
- Purchasing
- Consuming
- Disposing

Depending on community resources and need, local governments may be able to develop a collection of strategies across several elements of a food system that support the local economy and help meet food needs. Thinking of reducing hunger as one benefit of a local food system broadens the food system's potential appeal and adds an economic development incentive to address a wicked problem.

*Source*: Rick Morse, *Community Food Councils: Challenges and Opportunities*, UNC School of Government Webinar On-Demand (2014), www.sog.unc.edu/node/30976.

the structure and thoughtfully targeting participants give the local government a greater degree of control and allow it to use resources creatively.

Overall, the focus should be on bringing in a diverse array of partners and building relationships with them. Doing so allows a local government to broaden its perspective, think creatively about issues and how they affect multiple parts of the community, and expand the base of support for addressing wicked problems. Perhaps a private business in the community is interested in helping with environmental conservation efforts in order to reduce its energy costs. Maybe the local newspaper would like to help establish a program for improving student achievement in order to increase its readership among well-educated community members. Thinking broadly and describing efforts in ways that appeal to a wide variety of community members can help a local government create a customized local structure to combat wicked problems in measurable ways.

**WORKSHEET:** *Mapping Assets and Challenges for One Wicked Problem in Your Community*

Pick a wicked problem in your community. Who is interested in addressing this problem? Why are they interested?

_____

_____

_____

What other local organizations or people may be interested in addressing this problem? How can you appeal to them and align your goals with theirs?

_____

_____

_____

What is the history of action in your community on this problem? How does it affect the way you will address the issue?

_____

_____

_____

Who is affected by the problem but not engaged in the solution? How can you engage them?

_____

_____

_____

What are the strengths and challenges of those who are interested in solving the problem? How can you work together to produce stronger outcomes?

_____

_____

_____

How have other local governments addressed the same wicked problem you are facing? Can you learn from their experiences? How might you collaborate with them to address the problem?

_____

_____

_____

What regional, state, or federal government or philanthropic partners could help address this problem?

_____

_____

_____

Who are the key gatekeepers who can help you build collaborative relationships? How can you get them involved?

_____

_____

_____

What are the barriers to collaboration with any of the groups you listed above? How can you overcome these barriers?

_____

_____

_____

## ▶ Guiding Principle Number 2: *Government is well positioned to be a convener of efforts.*

The second major characteristic of wicked problems is that they are cross-cutting. Because they affect many sectors of a community and are not easily addressed in just one area, wicked problems require coordinated efforts from a variety of players. As discussed in the section above, identifying interested groups and aligning efforts in a community are central to devising a strategy to address a wicked problem. If efforts are not aligned, independent actions to combat a wicked problem may simply cause the problem to appear in a different part of the community. Consider the whack-a-mole game, in which a player uses a mallet to hit moles as they pop up from the holes in the game console. It is difficult for one player to react quickly and hit all the moles that pop up. However, if a number of players were involved, it would be much easier to whack the moles. Attacking wicked problems is similarly more effective with coordinated action among a variety of stakeholders.

Once the various stakeholders are identified, the next course of action is to define what the group hopes to accomplish. However, local leaders must first answer some other questions. What roles should the various groups play? How will the disparate groups work together? What resources are available, and how will they be used? Which groups are best positioned to deliver services?

Playing the role of convener can be difficult, but local governments are in an excellent position to do so. They are familiar with community nonprofits, have access to state and federal government resources, and broadly represent their local communities. They are also often able to coordinate action among various groups. Appendix A of this guidebook provides a list of key issues to think through when bringing stakeholders together and defining mutual expectations.

This unique position creates great opportunities for local governments. Convening stakeholders, clarifying roles, coordinating action, and sharing information are integral to success in addressing wicked problems. Governments can play coordinating roles without being involved directly in service delivery, and they can provide needed resources without overtaxing local government personnel. Figure 1 provides a spectrum of government involvement to give local governments a basic framework for thinking about how active they can be when addressing wicked problems.

When convening efforts, it is important to decide at the outset who will lead the charge. This decision should be based on the knowledge, resources, and willingness of the stakeholders. If the local government is in the best position to step up and coordinate or lead group efforts, a more active role involving local government personnel will be required. However, other stakeholders often have more knowledge of a problem and the ability to take a leading role. In that case, the local government can assist in the effort by providing

## Figure 1.   A Spectrum of Government Involvement

The spectrum below shows categories of government involvement in tackling wicked problems. The examples in this guidebook tend to fall in the "convene" and "coordinate" categories, but all levels of government involvement have benefits for communities.

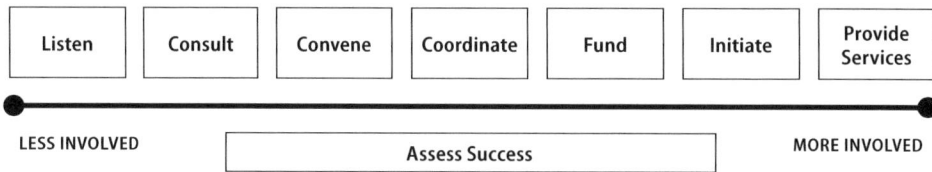

| Listen | Consult | Convene | Coordinate | Fund | Initiate | Provide Services |
|--------|---------|---------|------------|------|----------|------------------|

**LESS INVOLVED**                        Assess Success                        **MORE INVOLVED**

For further examples of how to engage along this spectrum, see John B. Stephens, Ricardo S. Morse, and Kelley T. O'Brien, *Public Outreach and Participation* (UNC School of Government, 2011).

resources that allow existing groups and programs to function more efficiently. A welcome outcome of such assistance may be that it reduces the need for the government to provide services directly.

It is often helpful to assign co-leaders to ensure that each group's voice is heard. Collaborative leadership can help keep the various groups focused and committed over the long term. It may also help participants maintain momentum across the board and flexibly use resources to meet the needs of all stakeholders.

To play the role of convener and facilitator, local governments need to define the collaborative relationship among the various groups. To address wicked problems, all levels need to appreciate and respect the roles played by the others without staking out turf or attempting to dominate in certain areas, and all of the players must be willing to work as a team. Dividing leadership among partners can help ensure that the group remains focused and committed over the long term.

It is helpful to think of the cross-cutting nature of collaboration in terms of vertical relationships and horizontal relationships. In vertical collaboration, the local government may need to take on a lead role, even if it is primarily as the convener or coordinator. In horizontal coordination, the local government is well positioned to bring together community players, such as faith-based organizations, independent nonprofits, businesses, and other areas of government.

Horizontal collaboration is different from vertical collaboration in that potential partners are assumed to be joining the effort from a relatively equal power position, although this assumption should be tested repeatedly to ensure that all interested groups have a voice in decision making. Partnering horizontally in a way that fits the local situation can broaden support for action and help meet the needs of a variety of stakeholders in

## Vertical and Horizontal Collaborative Efforts to Combat Hunger

In North Carolina, both the Department of Public Instruction (DPI) and the Department of Health and Human Services (DHHS) provide summer meals programs for children. While both programs serve children eligible for free and reduced-price school meals during the school year and both provide the same services, they are parallel programs administered separately by different state agencies.[a] Participation in each program is low. According to state officials and community partners familiar with the two programs, the primary obstacles to participation are inadequate funding for program implementation, inability to transport meals and/or children to feeding sites, and the overall burden of administering the programs.

To overcome these obstacles, the statewide nonprofit No Kid Hungry NC partnered with DPI and DHHS in an effort to increase participation in both summer meals programs through a pilot program called the Super Summer Meals Pilot. The pilot included collaboration that was both vertical and horizontal. Federal agencies provided assistance to state agencies, which then provided assistance to local partners, and local schools and nonprofits worked together. Schools took on the paperwork burden and cooked the food because their staffs brought skills and experience in these areas to the table. Nonprofit partners helped distribute the food to the children scattered in different locations during the summer. A few months after conceiving the idea of combining the programs, DPI and DHHS wrote and submitted a formal proposal to the US Department of Agriculture. Approval came soon after, and the pilot ran in eleven locations across North Carolina during the summer of 2012.

a. Legislation passed in 2014 transfers the North Carolina Summer Food Service Program from the Department of Health and Human Services to the Department of Public Instruction, placing both programs under the same roof for the first time. The change is effective October 1, 2014. S.L. 2014-100 (S 744), sec. 12E.9.(a)–(b).

a community. Imagine the multiplier effect if a local government is able to convene the resources of, for example, faith communities, focused interest groups, and businesses to combat a wicked problem that it does not have the resources to address on its own.

Although local governments are often well positioned to take an active role in addressing wicked problems, there may still be challenges. By its nature, local government can bring bureaucratic and political baggage with it. Lack of trust can undermine collaboration. Political conditions can redirect local government leaders' attention to new issues, or elections can bring in new leaders with different focus areas. Nonprofit partners and businesses can also decide to change direction and drop out of group efforts. Challenges like these are not trivial, and it is important for local government leaders to assess the overall value of playing an active and/or central role in addressing wicked problems. With careful planning and long-term commitment to combining the steadiness of the institution of government with the energy of interested local partners, many challenges can be overcome.

**WORKSHEET:** *Taking Action to Address Wicked Problems*

*Building on your answers from the worksheet on page 15, answer the following questions with the same wicked problem in mind.*

How does your organization currently engage with other groups to address the wicked problem? What goals does your organization have for mitigating this problem? How do your goals align with those of other groups?

_____

_____

_____

Which governmental departments have either a direct or an indirect interest in addressing the wicked problem? Who within your government is positioned to coordinate activities among the public, nonprofit, and private sectors?

_____

_____

_____

How can existing structures be used to take action on the wicked problem? How can established systems be used in new ways to remove barriers between groups?

_____

_____

_____

Which professional or faith-based organizations are interested in addressing the wicked problem? How can you bring them into collaborative efforts?

_____

_____

_____

What relationships with other members of your community could be used to address the wicked problem? How could you build relationships with other groups that might be interested in addressing the problem but are not currently represented?

_____

_____

_____

Are there collaborative structures in place in your community to help different sectors work together? What are ways your government can use, supplement, or replicate those structures in order to address the wicked problem?

_____

_____

_____

How can you help connect parties interested in addressing the wicked problem in order to coordinate efforts?

_____

_____

_____

Do you have access to someone with facilitation skills to help design and guide initial efforts? What tools do you have to aid in effective coordination?

_____

_____

_____

## ► Guiding Principle Number 3: *Aim to shrink the problem and be willing to adjust over time.*

Finally, wicked problems are relentless by nature, often shifting over time. There are no magical solutions. Taking action to address wicked problems requires the coordinated efforts of a variety of stakeholders over a long period, even when it seems as if no progress is being made. Because of this, local governments should focus on shrinking the problem over time instead of solving it in the short term.

Often, a collection of microstrategies implemented in tandem can be more effective than one overarching plan. Microstrategies are actions taken in a short period of time that can be adjusted as needs change. These strategies employ a variety of small actions, rather than a major shift in strategy, to move toward a long-term goal. Using a collection of microstrategies is important in addressing wicked problems, because success in addressing one aspect of a problem can lead to new problems to solve. For example, creating emergency housing resources for the homeless might be a big win for a local government, but transitioning

### Setting Reasonable Goals for Summer Meals

Combating hunger is a daunting task. Setting reasonable goals for attacking the problem that do not seem unachievable is critical.

Entities in North Carolina identified increasing participation in summer meals programs for students as a reasonable way to address hunger. To improve participation, leaders focused on increasing both the number of participating groups around the state and the number of meals served by groups that were already participating. Setting goals in this manner allowed each locality to be flexible and meet the needs of its own community.

The chart below shows that even though the net number of sponsors providing meals increased by only eight, child attendance per day increased by more than four thousand. Setting dual reasonable goals enabled each community to enhance the impact of the program in a way that met local needs and increased overall participation.

**North Carolina Summer Meals Program Participation**

|  | 2012 | 2013 |
| --- | --- | --- |
| Number of sponsors | 118 | 126 |
| Average daily attendance | 93,850 | 98,420 |

individuals to long-term stable housing becomes the new problem. It is important to recognize such realities and be willing to shift strategies as needs evolve. Committed local government leaders must be willing to wield different methods at different times.

Local governments are well positioned to lead long-term efforts due to their stable position in the community—government is always there. However, control of government changes hands, political values shift, and the will to address a given problem may fade. Local government leadership and personnel also change over time. It is critical for current leaders to know what actions have been taken in the past and to realize that they may need to tweak strategies and use a combination of methods to continue to address the problem. Leaders also need to consider how they are setting up their communities to combat problems moving forward.

It is important to measure the effects of past actions in order to adapt over the long term. But progress against wicked problems is difficult to measure, and many questions may arise. What represents success in addressing wicked problems? Are present efforts leading to success? How should stakeholders react to the data being gathered?

Using a "shrink the problem" approach that includes microstrategies allows local governments and their partners to gather data and measure success. This approach enables groups to cope with changes in the local environment and adapt as new problems emerge. It also allows them to be flexible with the strategies they employ to address the wicked problem.

To put this approach into practice, groups should develop reasonable goals for several measures of success for the problem they plan to address. Reporting on multiple measures can reveal how the microstrategies build on one another and can help the group focus on collective successes and challenges. In this way, groups can refocus their efforts slightly without abandoning the overall goal of reducing the effects of the wicked problem on the community. A multi-focused approach also allows groups to be more creative in the actions they take.

Coping with the relentless nature of wicked problems is a great challenge. Local governments can respond by setting reasonable and achievable goals and being flexible over time to meet these goals. Setting reasonable goals allows a local government to be accountable and measure progress, but it also takes into account the challenges inherent in addressing wicked problems. Being flexible allows a local government to take advantage of opportunities—such as new resources in the community—as they arise. And, when strategies are successful, flexibility allows a local government to increase its focus on the methods that are working without losing sight of the long-term goal.

*Building on your answers from the worksheet on page 20, answer the questions below with the same wicked problem in mind.*

What data exist on the wicked problem your community is facing? How does your organization use data to inform decision making?

_____

_____

_____

What are your long-term goals for mitigating the wicked problem?

_____

_____

_____

Based on the current characteristics and needs of your local community, where can you begin to address the wicked problem?

_____

_____

_____

What are a few measures that will show whether the actions you are taking are working?

_____

_____

_____

What reasonable goals can you set for these measures?

_____

_____

_____

Who is best positioned to collect and interpret data once you take action? How will you collect data to ensure that you are adapting to community needs?

_____

_____

_____

# Planning to Address Wicked Problems

Once local government leaders understand the three guiding principles, they can apply them as they plan to address wicked problems. Applying the principles strategically is central to ensuring that efforts to combat a wicked problem are sufficiently adapted to the specific nature of the problem. For this reason, it is appropriate to turn to a strategic planning framework.

Almost all organizations, including local governments, have gone through some sort of strategic planning. This process can help local a government organize its plan of attack for a wicked problem. Strategic planning allows the local government to define the scope of the problem, identify areas of strength, and coordinate action among stakeholders. It can also provide a long-term vehicle for assessing progress and making changes. A formal strategic planning process to address wicked problems is not required, but using this concept can help local government leaders focus their thoughts as they plan to take action.

Although any strategic planning framework can be helpful, the discussion below is based on the School of Government's strategic planning model (see Figure 2).[1] This section applies the three guiding principles outlined above to the three key stages of the strategic planning process: envision, enact, and evaluate. Additionally, Appendix B of this guidebook provides a table mapping wicked problems to the stages of strategic planning.

Throughout any strategic planning process, it is important to remember that wicked problems are unstructured, cross-cutting, and relentless. Designing specific strategies based on these characteristics of wicked problems will lead to greater impact over the long term.

---

1. The Public Intersection Project at the School of Government can also advise and consult on specific uses for strategic planning. Contact Margaret Henderson (margaret@sog.unc.edu) or Lydian Altman (lydian@sog.unc.edu) for additional information.

## Figure 2. Strategic Public Leadership: Setting Priorities and Getting Results

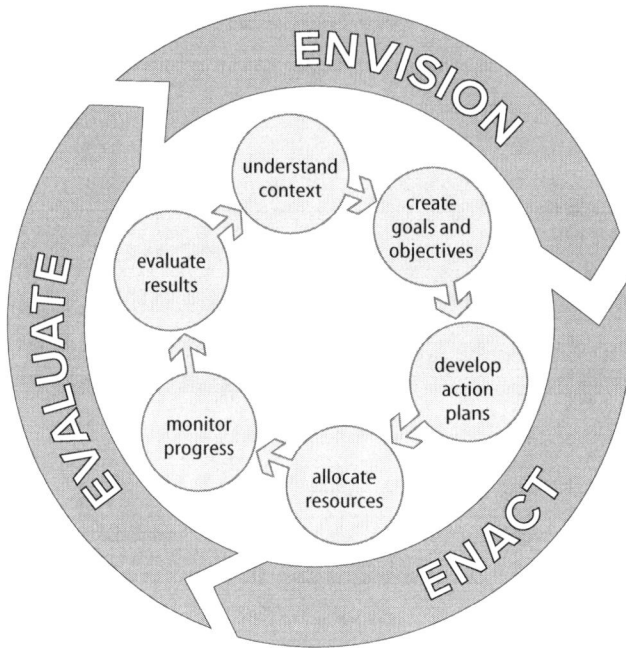

## Envision

Creating a shared understanding of issues and goals is important in addressing any problem (see Figure 3). Taking time on this step lays the groundwork for future success. However, this can be extremely difficult when the problem is a wicked one. Because they are complex and affect communities in many different areas, envisioning wicked problems in

## Figure 3. Where Do We Want to Be?

*Bring stakeholders to the table.*

*Take the time to understand the community's unique needs.*

*Create reasonable objectives and devise strategies to meet them over the long term.*

productive ways is challenging. Keeping the guiding principles in mind provides a good starting point.

▶ *You don't govern alone. Work across boundaries to maximize all available resources.*
This is the most important principle for envisioning potential solutions to wicked problems. These problems involve many stakeholders, and identifying and combining stakeholders' motivations and efforts can be difficult. However, it is critical to think expansively when identifying potential partners. Involving representatives from diverse areas of the community can increase the opportunity for locating potential partners and resources.

Understanding the context of a wicked problem is crucial to planning how to attack it. Engaging those affected by the problem along with other stakeholders can bring to light differing perspectives on the issues to be addressed. Building a shared understanding of the problem ensures that all partners are on the same page when planning action.

Creating a shared vision of results is also important. For example, addressing transportation issues could involve developing walkable communities, improving access to public transportation, building new roads, or a combination of any number of items, each undertaken by a different entity. Engaging those affected by the problem throughout the process and working with a variety of stakeholders to envision common goals help inform decision making and choices among strategies. The shared vision can be used as a guide for addressing wicked problems and achieving the community's long-term goals.

▶ *Government is well positioned to be a convener of efforts.*
Local governments are well positioned to coordinate visioning efforts. They can usually provide meeting space, bring stakeholders together, and lend an organizing presence. Due to their authority and influence, government leaders can shape the direction of efforts, ensuring that all concerns are addressed. However, solutions should not be brainstormed in isolation, nor should they be fully implemented by government personnel. As a convener, a local government can help partners focus on shared assessments of individual and collective strengths and challenges. Each interested party brings different qualities to any effort to address a problem. Artfully guiding partners to a shared understanding of the wicked problem and facilitating group action are critical roles of the convener.

▶ *Aim to shrink the problem, and be willing to adjust over time.*
Attempts to solve wicked problems immediately or over short time spans generally set the stage for failure. It is also unrealistic to believe that the same strategy will continue to work over time. In addressing wicked problems, local governments and other players should attempt to shrink the problem by coming up with microstrategies that focus on reasonable

## The Importance of Creating a Shared Vision and Understanding

Ending hunger is an ambitious goal. The *Washington Post* asked leaders combating hunger to give their opinions on whether that goal was achievable. In the following excerpt, Nancy Roman, president and chief executive of the Capital Area Food Bank (capitalareafoodbank.org), discusses the importance of understanding the problem.

> *I don't believe the business community can end hunger all by itself. Neither can government. Neither can the Capital Area Food Bank. Hunger is a solvable problem. If the capital city of the richest country in the world links arms with the business community, with the nonprofit sector, with government, with individuals and society, yes, I think we can solve hunger Zip code by Zip code all across the Greater Washington area.*
>
> *So many people focus on fundraising. So do we. Funds matter. But one of the biggest things that has to happen is understanding. Understanding the role hunger plays in a society. Hunger underpins health, education [sic]. Understanding the incredible link between food and diet-related disease, and food and overall wellness. Understand where hunger is in your own community if you're a business. One of the things I've been struck by coming from the global scene is, it's easy for people to imagine hunger in Africa. It's hard for people to imagine hunger in Montgomery County or Fairfax County or a mile from the Capitol but there is hunger in all those places. A business starts by understanding the role of hunger. They have an interest in having a society of people who are well fed and well nourished. Understanding is the most critical first step. Once the understanding is there then every business has a different way of engaging. Some provide food, in-kind services, money, needed volunteers, critical partnership. Businesses educating their own employee base and what can be done is a real service. It's a complicated problem to get at the root of but there is no shortage of things that can be done.*

*Source*: Vanessa Small, "Can the Washington business community end hunger in this region? It depends who you ask," Capital Business (blog), *Washington Post*, November 24, 2013, www.washingtonpost.com/business/capitalbusiness/can-the-washington-business-community-end-hunger-in-this-region-it-depends-who-you-ask/2013/11/22/4903a5d8-5078-11e3-a7f0-b790929232e1_story.html. Reprinted by permission.

## Understanding the Community's Unique Needs and Strengths

When deciding whether to offer summer meals, communities in North Carolina have several options. Some opt not to provide meals, some opt for meals served only at schools, and some choose to serve meals wherever the children are located. Each approach varies in cost and effectiveness depending on the situation, and even the geography, of each school district. For example, Kannapolis is a small city and chooses to serve summer meals only at central locations that are easily accessible. In contrast, Gaston County prepares food for summer meals in a central kitchen and delivers it to sites around the county, such as schools, libraries, and mobile home parks.

Each leader in the summer meals program assesses its community's unique needs and strengths when deciding upon the size and scope of the local program. This increases the effectiveness of efforts and the likelihood of making short-term gains that maintain momentum.

## External and Community Definitions of Success

In 2012, the newly implemented Super Summer Meals Pilot was a success in terms of the standard federal reporting measure of July attendance. In North Carolina, however, there has historically been a large drop off in attendance at summer meal sites in August. With this in mind, program participants set a local goal of increasing August participation in 2013.

Each participant developed localized strategies to maintain momentum in the feeding program throughout the entire summer. Some chose to partner with new nonprofits to serve meals in August, while others extended service through existing partnerships by a week or two.

As illustrated in the table below, the program made major advances in meeting its goal, even though it was not critical for federal reporting requirements. August attendance at summer meals sites in 2013 increased by more than 30,000 children per day.

### North Carolina Summer Meals Program Participation

|  | 2012 | 2013 |
|---|---|---|
| July average daily attendance | 108,630 | 116,515 |
| August average daily attendance | 62,286 | 92,799 |

goals and make the problem more manageable. Envisioning the process of addressing wicked problems in terms of chipping away at an iceberg can help keep expectations realistic and lead to measurable success both in the short term and over time.

It is also important to keep a flexible mindset. Remaining open to change will allow the group to react to new ideas, resources, or limitations and adjust as necessary by scaling up successful strategies while tweaking or eliminating those that are less effective.

## QUESTIONS FOR DISCUSSION: *Getting Started on a Shared Vision*

1. What is your vision for your community's wicked problem? Why is it important that your organization act on this problem?

2. How are you defining the problem? What limits or boundaries does this definition create for the organization's efforts? How can you overcome these barriers?

3. Who should be involved to help you further envision the problem? How will you gather input from constituents and other groups?

4. Who are the stakeholders you can identify to help generate ideas? How can you involve new partners to develop creative solutions?

5. What are your individual and collective assets? How can you structure your action to use these assets effectively and efficiently?

6. How do the three guiding principles affect your thinking in the envisioning stage of strategic planning? What reasonable goals can you set?

7. What examples can you use from other communities to help you envision your action?

## Enact

Putting microstrategies into action presents its own set of challenges. However, enacting is the most straightforward part of addressing wicked problems, and it should be the easiest portion to conceptualize (see Figure 4). Keeping the guiding principles in mind during group activities such as meetings and retreats and connecting microstrategies to budget items can help local governments enact strategies effectively.

**Figure 4.  How Do We Put Our Goals into Action?**

ENACT

*Develop roles for all stakeholders.*

*Share information regularly and ensure that stakeholders stay on the same page.*

*Be willing to adjust strategies as you implement.*

▶ *You don't govern alone. Work across boundaries to maximize all available resources.*

Using a variety of stakeholders to attack a wicked problem allows each partner to play a distinct role. This increases the capacity of the entire team and allows each group to focus on its assets and strengths. With multiple stakeholders involved, the group can tackle bigger problems and deploy more financial and human resources to address them.

Once various stakeholders have been identified and recruited, keeping them involved is critical. Working across boundaries between the various groups will help ensure consistent action and communication. Building relationships and support will help keep all of the parties on the same page, and communicating effectively and often will help prevent duplication of efforts. Sharing information regularly and seeking feedback on progress can help each stakeholder improve its efforts.

## Combining Services through Nonprofits to Increase Access

At the food pantry at St. Joseph's Catholic Church in Burgaw, NC, the Food and Nutrition Services Outreach Coordinator for the Wilmington Branch of the Food Bank of Central and Eastern NC comes to the pantry to assist clients with applying for Supplemental Nutrition Assistance Program (SNAP) benefits. When people check in at the start of each visit, they are asked by volunteers if they receive SNAP benefits, and if they do not, they are told that they can apply on-site with the outreach coordinator. In addition to the outreach coordinator, the pantry also has a Spanish-speaking caseworker from Catholic Charities to assist clients.

In Wilson, NC, the state Department of Agriculture, the county departments of social services and public health, the sheriff's office, and a local nonprofit all come together once a quarter to distribute food, provide free health screenings, and determine eligibility for work training programs implemented by the nonprofit.

In both Wilson and Burgaw, each entity could have acted alone and been less effective while addressing the same problems. By breaking down barriers and combining resources, these communities were able to improve services for citizens and turn their individual goals into a shared vision.

Local food banks and faith-based organizations often provide needed services to community members. Harnessing and combining their existing efforts with those of local government can increase the impact of programs and strategies. *Details*: Sister Brenda Johnson, Recruiters for Christ Pantry—Raleigh Branch of the Food Bank of Central & Eastern North Carolina. *Source: Feeding Our State—A Portrait of Hunger in North Carolina.*

Donn Young Photography

---

**Partnering with Local Nonprofits to Address Hunger**

In Durham County, the volume of meals served in the summer meals program is very high. To meet this need, the school district partners with a variety of outside organizations that are not school related, and almost 80 percent of the sites at which meals are served are not schools.

The school district delivers meals each day to local churches and nonprofits, which then serve the meals to children. This enables the school district to reduce its budget burden by using volunteer labor from local partners to serve more than 5,000 meals a day during the summer months. While the school district maintains responsibility for the program and reporting, it is able to coordinate efforts to increase the overall coverage area and feed more needy children. The school district is also able to share information about successes and challenges at each individual site with a variety of partners, thus ensuring that each group has all the information it needs to feed as many children as possible.

---

▶ *Government is well positioned to be a convener of efforts.*

Despite local government's key position, it is not necessary for the government to undertake all of the efforts itself. Coordinating strategies, regularly communicating across boundaries, and connecting various players are also important roles local governments can play in order to keep efforts on track and maintain momentum. Sharing success stories and challenges with all interested parties is another way that local governments can contribute to the process. In particular, thoughtful media outreach can help celebrate success and draw new interested groups into the effort.

Addressing wicked problems is hard work. Having a convener to keep everyone moving in the same direction can go a long way toward ensuring long-term success.

▶ *Aim to shrink the problem and be willing to adjust over time.*

Even when microstrategies are employed, shifting course is common in addressing wicked problems. Keeping this in mind can help participants stay motivated. Challenges will arise along the way, and being willing to adjust both in the short term and over time is a key aspect of successful strategic intervention. Flexibility and exploration of a variety of strategies allow local governments and stakeholders to meet both shared and individual goals.

Again, communication is essential. Newsletters, meetings, and positive media stories can help stakeholders focus on their successes in chipping away at the iceberg of wicked problems. Combining the experience of all participants into one narrative can build a sense of shared purpose and ownership and increase stakeholders' willingness to adjust as successful strategies emerge. As a convener and stable leader, a local government can encourage communication and help the group maintain momentum.

## Adjusting the Meals Program for Spanish Speakers

Summer meals officials in Brunswick County, NC, knew that there was a large population of Spanish-speaking children who were not being fed. When the lunch buses went to predominantly Hispanic neighborhoods, the children disappeared.

The solution to the problem was a simple poster. No Kid Hungry NC provided each school district with posters in both Spanish and English, encouraging parents to engage with summer meals providers when the lunch buses arrived in their neighborhood. Although the meals providers did not speak Spanish and the parents did not speak English, they were able to break through a barrier and ensure that the children received the meals. Sharing and replicating simple strategies like this can have a large impact on wicked problems.

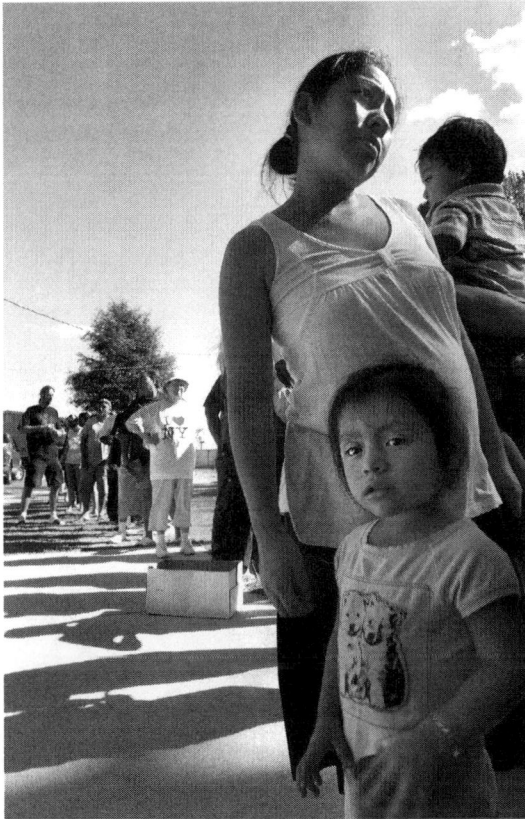

Some community members may not have access to programs designed to meet their needs. By engaging leaders in their own small communities, local governments can help provide services to larger and more diverse groups of constituents. *Details*: Recruiters for Christ Pantry—Dunn, NC. *Source: Feeding Our State—A Portrait of Hunger in North Carolina.*

Donn Young Photography

**QUESTIONS FOR DISCUSSION:** *Taking Action and Maintaining Momentum*

1. What should your organization be responsible for doing? What resources/policies are needed to take action?

2. How will your governing board and senior leaders communicate with others to maintain coordination and momentum on wicked problems? What committees do you have in place? What presentations do you invite? What forums do you offer? Are there other creative ways that you can communicate successes and challenges?

3. How will you ensure that all participants maintain the same focus? What structures can you use to keep communication open and clear?

4. How can you encourage all participants to communicate both formal and informal successes and challenges?

5. How will you react to successes? What can you do to replicate and scale up success?

6. How will you react to challenges? What criteria will you use to determine whether strategies should be adjusted?

## Evaluate

Measuring success and planning for improvement is the third step in strategic planning (see Figure 5). Because wicked problems are cross-cutting, it is often difficult to evaluate successes and challenges associated with actions in multiple areas. Choosing a few key measures and focusing on reasonable goals, while also recognizing that goals may change, are important in evaluating actions taken against wicked problems. Using the guiding principles helps ensure that accountability is shared among participants, momentum is sustained, and problems are addressed practically.

**Figure 5.   How Can We Integrate and Align Evaluation?**

> EVALUATE

*Evaluate efforts in a way that all stakeholders trust.*

*Use formal and informal evaluation to focus efforts on key issues.*

*Note successes and challenges in order to continue to improve.*

► *You don't govern alone. Work across boundaries to maximize all available resources.*

In terms of evaluation, this means managing accountability among the various participants addressing the wicked problem. Working collaboratively with partners, governments can establish an accountability framework that distributes responsibility among all parties. Because different groups will have different interests, it is important to ensure that a party respected by all groups prepares a complete and competent evaluation.

Not all groups have to accept and use the same measures of accountability. Instead, each group should use whatever measures are necessary to accommodate its specific needs. There may be multiple measures of success, and even if the short-term goals of each group are different, the long-term goal of reducing the impact of wicked problems can still be attained. It is important to keep in mind, however, that no matter what the measures, trust and objectivity are critical to ensuring that all parties respect the evaluation process and the ensuing results.

Trusted, well-planned, and in-depth evaluation can break down barriers among participants and collaborators and help all parties use resources more effectively. A comprehensive evaluation also allows different stakeholders to use the information that is most important for their own decision making without limiting or manipulating the big picture. Whether participants engage an outside evaluator, employ a collaborative internal approach, or choose one stakeholder with the skills and expertise necessary to provide an evaluation, planning for evaluation from the beginning helps ensure that all groups have access to the information they need.

► *Government is well positioned to be a convener of efforts.*

Local governments are well positioned to play a key role in the evaluation of efforts and responses to concerns. They are usually more familiar with gathering data and using evaluation to improve services than are nonprofits. Even if a local government does not have staff members who are familiar with evaluation, it may have connections to other partners who have those skills. Ongoing evaluation efforts by local government or another key group may also encourage other players to undertake their own evaluations. Periodic analysis of progress also enables stakeholders to adjust their strategies over time.

It is important to anticipate that not all groups will be enthusiastic about evaluation, nor will they necessarily be prepared to do it. Some participants may even view evaluations as "gotcha" moments which only serve to justify predetermined ideas. However, evaluations can be user-friendly, and they need not be complex to be effective. One size seldom fits all, though, and conveners need to tailor evaluation tools to specific actions, taking care to make adjustments commensurate with the scope of service as it evolves.

**Trusted Evaluation of the Pilot Summer Meals Program**

In order to facilitate transparent evaluation, leaders of the summer meals pilot worked with the School of Government to complete a full evaluation of the program.[a] For No Kid Hungry NC, the evaluation needed to include an assessment of a texting feature being promoted by its national and state offices that allowed caregivers to find the closest source for free lunch meals for children. For the Department of Public Instruction, the evaluation needed to include feedback from its employees, the child nutrition administrators who participated. The Department of Health and Human Services was interested in how new approaches to program training for local partners were received. And everyone, from local partners to national stakeholders, wanted trustworthy numbers.

In this case, an outside organization with no involvement in the program's delivery and no stake in its success or failure, and with staff trained in evaluation, was needed to satisfy the combined needs of the stakeholders. The School of Government played this role.

The result was an evaluation that showed a dramatic increase in participation in the locations participating in the pilot program. However, had that been all the data reported, the pilot would have been misjudged. Qualitative data such as confidential, in-depth interviews revealed details that were also important to the program managers.

For the Super Summer Meals Pilot, an evaluation from an outside organization allowed each group to get the information it needed and enabled stakeholders and the collective group to base strategies for continued improvements on trusted data.

a. The report, *Evaluation of the 2012 North Carolina Super Summer Meals Pilot*, is available at http://sogpubs.unc.edu/electronicversions/pdfs/evalsummermealsrpt2013.pdf.

▶ *Aim to shrink the problem and be willing to adjust over time.*

Focusing on successes while adapting over time is key to addressing wicked problems. Results will not happen overnight, but stakeholders can take important steps in the short term that lay the foundation for long-term success. When evaluating strategic actions, it is important to note both successes and challenges to ensure that all groups continue to improve their strategies.

A consistent presence is necessary to keep stakeholders focused on the long-term goal of shrinking the wicked problem. Local governments are also well positioned to play this role due to their stable position the community. Local governments are able to weather turnover in nonprofit personnel, stay abreast of changes in regulations from state and federal governments, identify new funding opportunities, and adjust to changes in their communities. Even if the composition of a local government changes, its policy focus shifts, or its capacity is reduced, it can still enhance efforts to address wicked problems by serving as a listener

## Using a Working Group to Perform Informal Assessment

To ensure that the summer meals program continues to improve, the state's Department of Health and Human Services (DHHS) organized an informal working group that meets regularly to discuss plans for the summer meals program. Comprising individuals from school districts, local food pantries and nonprofits, and DHHS, the working group serves as a forum for stakeholders to share their stories. DHHS typically provides meeting space and a box lunch and shares statewide program data.

The group provides on-the-ground assessment of successes and challenges and helps shape future strategies. Some members of the group are long term and some are new. Some members are fully committed to the program and others are more ambivalent about it. These diverse points of view help the group assess the program honestly.

Open communication facilitated by a government agency can be a crucial factor in evaluating the success of programs that attack wicked problems. This communication allows all interested parties to work toward common solutions.

and consultant. It can also provide meeting space, generate ideas based on its experience with the community, and provide relevant data to allow stakeholders to evaluate progress.

The local context for wicked problems and evaluation techniques may change over time, but the need to shrink wicked problems does not. Keeping stakeholders' sights on measuring success in the short term is critical to making an impact over the long term.

## Identifying Successes and Challenges in Summer Meals Delivery

When the School of Government completed the evaluation of the summer meals program, results were largely positive. However, some areas needed improvement. Specifically, the administrative burden of paperwork and reporting required participants to spend more time and energy completing paperwork than feeding children. With this in mind, the group developed strategies to build upon successes and adjust the program to address challenges.

Group leaders wanted to expand the program where possible. While efforts were under way to start up new programs in areas with no service, leaders determined that expanding participation county-by-county and city-by-city could provide more meals to needy children at little additional cost. In other words, the group might be able to accomplish more overall simply by focusing on expanding in areas where providers had experience and the political, physical, and social infrastructure was already in place. To help mitigate the paperwork burden, the Department of Agriculture granted schools in good standing with the National School Lunch Program a more streamlined application, monitoring, and documentation process. This allowed providers to spend more time feeding kids and less time filling out forms.

**QUESTIONS FOR DISCUSSION:** *Evaluating Action to Adjust Strategies*

1. How will you evaluate the success of your actions? Who will be involved in the evaluation?

2. How often will you evaluate your success? How will you use the information you gathered to restart the strategic planning process for wicked problems?

3. How will you adjust your next plan based on the evaluation? How will you consult all involved participants to discuss their future participation?

# Conclusion

Wicked problems are difficult to address. They defy traditional approaches to problem solving and remain entrenched over time. Nevertheless, the interconnected nature of problems in today's society means that governments must be prepared and willing to combat wicked problems. The problems may not be eradicated in a year, or maybe even in a decade, but actions taken now can have large effects down the road.

Local governments are close to their constituents and well positioned to respond to the needs of their communities. Using the three guiding principles in conjunction with the strategic planning process described in this guidebook, local governments can play a key role in addressing wicked problems.

---

### Planning for Future Summer Meals Efforts

Local leaders in North Carolina continue to make efforts to attack hunger. Cities, towns, counties, nonprofits, churches, and schools across the state are committed to combating the problem. This summer, local leaders plan to implement the creative solution of retrofitting buses to serve as mobile cafeterias. They plan to continue bilingual outreach efforts. And they plan to work with one another to maximize resources by expanding their network of nonprofit and government partners. In these and other ways, North Carolina's local leaders will continue to address hunger and other wicked problems in their communities.

***Appendix C of this guidebook provides resources for addressing hunger.***

# Additional Resources

Henderson, Margaret, Lydian Altman, Suzanne Julian, Gordon P. Whitaker, and Eileen Youens. *Working with Nonprofit Organizations.* Chapel Hill, NC: UNC School of Government, 2010.

Stephens, John B., Ricardo S. Morse, and Kelley T. O'Brien. *Public Outreach and Participation.* Chapel Hill, NC: UNC School of Government, 2011.

UNC School of Government. *Community and Economic Development in North Carolina and Beyond.* ced.sog.unc.edu.

Development finance tools can be used in creative ways to combat wicked problems. The UNC School of Government provides specialized finance and development expertise, with the goal of enabling local governments and their partners to accomplish their community and economic development goals. For more information, contact Tyler Mulligan at the UNC School of Government (mulligan@sog.unc.edu).

UNC School of Government. *Public Intersection Project.* www.publicintersection.unc.edu.

The *Public Intersection Project* at the School of Government can advise and consult on specific uses for strategic planning. For more information, contact Margaret Henderson (margaret@sog.unc.edu) or Lydian Altman (lydian@sog.unc.edu).

# Appendix A: Defining (or Redefining) Mutual Expectations in a Collaborative Relationship

The guide below provides key questions for stakeholders to think through in planning to address wicked problems collaboratively.

1. What is the overall purpose of this relationship?
2. What specifically do you hope to accomplish by having this relationship? Consider benefits for both members of the group and any stakeholders outside the group.
   - Communication
   - Interaction
   - Tasks
   - Events
   - Products
   - Processes
   - Other outcomes
3. Who can or should participate regularly in this group's meetings?
   - Are there others who can or should periodically participate in meetings or provide feedback to guide the actions of this group?
   - Will leadership be assigned or rotated?
   - Who can bring issues to the group's attention through either the formal agenda or informal discussion?
4. Who is expected to carry out which actions, and for whom?
   - Logistical arrangements for convening meetings
   - Financial management
   - Communicating with group members or external stakeholders
   - Implementing new or revised service or support activities

5. Who can invoke or alter these expectations? Under what circumstances?

6. How will decisions be made within the group?
   - About the group
   - About group finances
   - About the group's service population or desired outcomes
   - About the group's joint or coordinated service or support activities

7. How will resources be shared or allocated?

8. How will the group report on its activities, responsibilities, or progress?
   - Content and format of information
   - Who collects the information?
   - Who prepares the information?
   - Who receives the information?
   - How can this information be used outside the group?

9. How will the group evaluate its success?

*Source*: UNC School of Government, *Public Intersection Project*, www.publicintersection.unc.edu.

# Appendix B: Wicked Problems Mapped to Stages of Strategic Planning

The table below breaks down wicked problems by characteristic and the strategic planning cycle by stage.

## Wicked Problems Mapped to Stages of Strategic Planning

| Strategic Planning Stage | Wicked Problems Are Unstructured, Cross-Cutting, and Relentless | | |
|---|---|---|---|
| | *Unstructured* | *Cross-Cutting* | *Relentless* |
| **Envision** | The challenge:<br>• Coming to consensus on a comprehensive and accurate definition of the problem. | The challenge:<br>• Identifying and convening all of the interested, informed, or connected stakeholders. | The challenge:<br>• Keeping the energy focused over the long haul. |
| | Coping strategy:<br>• Come to consensus on a functional, if limited, definition of the issue for this community at this time. | Coping strategy:<br>• Recognize that the problem-solving process will take more time and involve a greater investment of attention and resources than many public problems do. | Coping strategies:<br>• Invest in facilitative leadership.<br>• Plan for leadership transitions. |
| **Enact** | The challenge:<br>• There likely is no single comprehensive solution. | The challenge:<br>• No one holds all of the answers or all of the data that describe either the problem or the progress in implementing strategies. | The challenge:<br>• Preparing recordkeeping systems that are adaptable for very different types of strategies or service providers. |
| | Coping strategy:<br>• Develop an array of micro-strategies that address pieces of the problem. | Coping strategies:<br>• Create mutual agreements that define both the strategies to be implemented by any stakeholder and the data to be collected.<br>• Devise a central collection point for receiving and summarizing all of the programmatic data. | Coping strategies:<br>• Practice transparency in terms of defining expectations, assessing progress, and sharing information.<br>• Practice risk management by ensuring data are kept in a compatible format and stored in more than one place. |

*(continued)*

## Wicked Problems Mapped to Stages of Strategic Planning (*continued*)

| Strategic Planning Stage | Wicked Problems Are Unstructured, Cross-Cutting, and Relentless | | |
| --- | --- | --- | --- |
| | *Unstructured* | *Cross-Cutting* | *Relentless* |
| **Evaluate** | The challenge: <br> • It is likely impossible to collect all of the relevant data that apply to the problem or its solutions. | The challenge: <br> • Defining and upholding overly broad or one-size-fits-all expectations. | The challenge: <br> • Keeping up the effort over the long haul. |
| | Coping strategy: <br> • Define and collect key indicators that represent pieces of the problem. | Coping strategies: <br> • Separate out and formally agree to any collective expectations (such as expectations related to sharing information, resources, or decision making). <br> • Specify any individualized expectations for particular service providers or change agents. | Coping strategy: <br> • Define and assign responsibility, then allocate the necessary resources to a particular party in charge of collecting the data, conducting the assessments, and reporting the findings to all of the stakeholders. |

# Appendix C: Hunger Resources

For more information on addressing hunger, please visit the School of Government Hunger Research website at **hunger-research.sog.unc.edu**. The website provides data and quick facts on hunger in North Carolina, recent publications detailing how hunger affects people across the country, and resources for taking steps to reduce the effects of hunger in your community. Please contact Maureen Berner at the UNC School of Government (berner@sog.unc.edu) if you have further questions on the effects of hunger or are interested in exploring options to address hunger in your community.

The US Department of Agriculture defines food deserts as urban neighborhoods and rural towns without ready access to fresh, healthy, and affordable food. Instead of supermarkets and grocery stores, these communities have no food access or are served only by fast food restaurants and convenience stores that offer few healthy, affordable food options. The lack of access contributes to a poor diet and can lead to higher levels of obesity and other diet-related diseases, such as diabetes and heart disease. For more information, see United States Department of Agriculture, "Food Deserts," *Agriculture Marketing Service,* **http://apps.ams.usda.gov/fooddeserts/foodDeserts.aspx**.